The NO Book for Teenagers

By

Susan Louise Peterson

All rights reserved © 2013 by
Susan Louise Peterson

No part of this book may be reproduced
or transmitted in any form or by any
means, graphic, electronic, or mechanical,
including photocopying, recording,
taping, or by any information storage
retrieval system, without the written
permission of the publisher.

For information address:

Vilnius Press

244 Fifth Avenue

New York, NY 10001

Printed in the United States of America

CONTENTS

Foreword	ii
Preface	iv
Acknowledgements	v
Introduction	vi
Chapter 1 No Could Mean That a Change is Needed	1
Chapter 2 No Could Mean the Timing is Off	12
Chapter 3 No Could Mean There are Complications	23
Chapter 4 No Could Mean the Request is Not Really Appropriate	34
Chapter 5 No Could Mean There Are Safety Issues	45
Chapter 6 No Could Mean the Request is Not a Good Resource	57
Chapter 7 No Could Mean There is No Clear Direction	68
Chapter 8 No Could Mean More Reflection is Needed	79
Chapter 9 No Could Mean Learning New Lessons	90
Recommended Reading for Teenagers	101
Index	102
About the Author	104

FOREWORD

This year the day I turned 18 I thought, "I'm an adult now, I know everything!," boy was I wrong. Since then, I have come to terms that I still don't know everything, but it's okay. I have lots to learn, and plenty of time to do so. As a teenager, I believe that one of the biggest steps to maturity is knowing that you don't know everything, and taking responsibility for yourself and for others. I feel my parents have based all of their "No" answers on facts and their life experiences. The "No" answers have always been their way of trying to protect me and make me a better person as I mature. Sometimes it has been very frustrating. And since hindsight is 20/20, they have usually been right. I now understand.

Then there is this other interesting thing that my Mother has used to base a lot of her "No" answers. She calls it a "feeling in her chest" about this, that, or the other. I never understood it until recently. Fortunately now at 18 I think I finally get it and I too have learned how to listen to this amazing "feeling in your chest" thing. Most people ignore it. The best description I can give you is this....when you have all the information and you still just have a funny "feeling in your chest" that something is just not right... that is your instinct talking to you! Listen to it and do something! I now understand.

The No Book for Teenagers is an insight for teens trying to understand parents, who are having just as hard of time understanding their teens. "No", usually seems so rough, unforgiving, and negative, but is brought to a whole new light with the real wisdom and meaning behind our parent's words. The "No Book for Teenagers" is a vital link for teenagers, like you and me, to comprehend that when our parents say "this is for your own good", *it really is*. Trust me, I have found out that when parents say "I'm not trying to make you mad, I'm just trying to keep you safe", *they really are*. I feel at 18 I am becoming a better teenager to prepare for life as an adult because of all of the "No" answers. Thanks to my parents I am learning the boundaries of life. As hard as it may sound, I think we teenagers all need to accept the word "No". Help is here with the "No Book for Teenagers!"

Taylor Ware
National and International
Yodeling Champion

PREFACE

A teenager's life is filled with constant requests to go places, do things and ask for items. The common response from teachers and parents is usually 'no.' The 'no' response often stops the communication or causes major disagreements between the teenager and his or her parent or teacher because the teenager doesn't really understand the meaning behind the word 'no.' The word 'no' can be connected with many things.

Having worked as a school psychologist and educator for over 20 years I have noticed the response that many parents and educator's give to a teenager's request is the word 'no.' This book is written to explore the various meanings connected with a 'no' response. It is hoped that parents, educators and teenagers can gain a better understanding of each other through the examples in this book.

ACKNOWLEDGEMENTS

I am grateful to the many people who have influenced my life. My parents in Oklahoma taught me about 'no' and how it was important to learn the simple lessons of country farm life. My husband and twin daughters teach me about saying 'no' in a city environment that is fast paced with urban schools and quick requests.

I would like to thank two amazing athletes- Lance Daniel, a champion bull rider from Georgia and Eli Hager, a member of the National/World Water Ski Team for their comments on the book. A special thanks also goes to Morgan Thompson, 2012-2013- International DECA President for her leadership and professional attitude. She is a great role model for teens. A big thanks goes to Curtis Wetovick, the 2011 International Junior Auctioneer Champion who was able to share a comment for the book while going to college, working a campus job and preparing for an auction competition at the same time. A big thanks goes to Taylor Ware, a champion Yodeler who is super talented for writing the foreword of the book and sharing her insights. Vilnius Press, my publisher is always appreciated for their willingness to help authors finish their final writing projects.

INTRODUCTION

Have you ever thought why parents and teachers say 'no' to most of your requests? Often you might think these adults are just putting road blocks in the way of your plans and being difficult with your requests. However, as a teenager you may not always get the whole picture and understand why these adults are being so negative about your requests.

It has been my observation as a school psychologist and parent that the use of 'no' by adults can have many valuable meanings. 'No' can be used to explain that a request is inappropriate or complicated. Parents often say 'no' when there are safety concerns or the timing is off with a request. 'No' can be a response indicating the request is not a good resource or that change is needed. Parents and teachers are often helping you to see there is no clear direction in the request. However, most importantly the adults are trying to help you see that more reflection is needed on the request and that 'no' can just mean learning the lessons of life.

CHAPTER ONE

No could mean that a change is needed

No could mean that a change is needed so that you can continue your request. For example, saying 'no' might mean you should consider more options and look at the challenges before you change a plan. No could mean that it is an unhealthy request or one that involves bad habits. Sometimes parents may want you to slow down in a relationship or calm down and relax more about a decision. At other times, parents are wanting you to gain independence and they help you in clarifying confusing details as you make adjustments and learn how to be flexible in life.

No might mean consider all options before you change something

"No, you can't buy the first car you drive, because you haven't looked at the other cars."

"No, you are not allowed to buy the first prom dress you try on until you have shopped several stores."

"No, you cannot enroll in the course until you check out all of the courses on the selection list."

"No, you cannot take the life guard training until you check on the junior life saving class."

"No, you can't take the advanced class until you check out the basic requirements."

☙

No might mean that you need to calm down and relax

"No, you can't go to Julie's house until you calm down."

"No you aren't allowed to go to the scream-fright house if you are upset and crying because they won't let you in there."

"No, you can't go to the party until you rest and relax since it is a late night."

"No, you won't be able to give the speech until you relax and breathe deeply."

"No, you can't perform tonight until your relax and get prepared for the performance."

☯

No might mean that you are inflexible

"No, you can't buy only the expensive prom dress, you have to choose one in your parent's budget."

"No, you can't go to the movies unless you pick a PG-13 rated movie."

"No, you can't buy a new phone every year; you have to just upgrade the features on your old phone."

"No, you can't have a new computer because you don't have the proper connections installed at your house."

"No, you can't go to camp unless you look at all of the travel costs to get there."

No might mean you need to change bad habits

"No, you can't avoid brushing your teeth with braces or you will get cavities."

"No, you can't use the flat iron if you don't use heat protector on your hair first."

"No, you can't wear makeup, if you don't clean it off at night or it will break out your face."

"No, that dress is too short and you will be sent home again for breaking the school dress code."

"No, you can't take the backpack, you need to clean out the old papers or the backpack will be too heavy."

∞

No might mean you need to make an adjustment

"No, you can't go on the trip to Hawaii until you plan your transportation to and from each island."

"No, you can't make the new reservation until you cancel the other flight reservation."

"No, the senior trip won't work unless you get back a day early from the conference."

"No, the costume won't fit until you hem it and add the trim to your hat."

"No, you can't plan the party until you find a room to hold the event."

No might mean you need to gain independence

"No, you can't pay the car insurance until you get a part time job."

"No, I'm not going to the school; you need to talk to your teacher about the problem."

"No, you go ask the principal if it is 'OK' to plan the party."

"No, before you can graduate, you must check with the counselor to see if you are cleared to graduate."

"No, I'm not filling out the application for you as you need to apply for the scholarship yourself."

☙

No might mean the relationship needs to slow down

"No, you can't go out with someone you just met."

"No, you need to meet the coach and the assistants before you commit to the team."

"No, you don't volunteer for the position until you meet the director and find out the position description."

"No, you can't commit to driving a carload of kids you hardly know."

"No, you can't join the swim team across town since you don't know the swim coach and her vision for the team."

‍ ℘

No might mean there is confusion about the details

"No, you can't go to the party because you don't know where it takes place or where it is located."

"No, you can't wear blue jeans because I think it is uniform day on Tuesday."

"No, you can't stand in the end field because it is my understanding you could get hurt and you will be in the player's way."

"No, you aren't allowed to bring the cell phone to camp and I believe that was stated in the camp guidelines."

"No, you can't eat food in class as the custodians don't want to clean up your mess and the handbook prohibits it."

No might mean there are numerous challenges in your plan

"No, you can't afford the rent, tuition and the books on your savings."

"No, you can't buy the concert tickets or it will take the money you saved for the senior trip."

"No, you can't go to a college so far away as you lack transportation funds to fly home on college breaks."

"No, you can't buy the car and afford the car payments on your salary."

"No, you won't be able to enroll in two colleges at the same time in the same town as it would be too complicated."

ಖ

No might mean there is something "unhealthy" about your request

"No, you can't travel to Mexico without your shots or there is a change you could get very sick."

"No, you can't go out in 100 degree temperatures without water or fluids in your body."

"No, you can't tan at the pool without putting on sunscreen."

"No, you can't eat only macaroni and cheese for every meal, you need a balanced diet."

"No, you can't wear shorts on the ski trip; you need to dress in warm clothes."

☙

CHAPTER TWO
No could mean the timing is off

No could mean the timing is off for your request. This may involve a variety of time related issues. For example, there could be too many things at one time or too many events and activities scheduled at the same time. Some of the activities may have bad timing and there is shortness of time to complete the task. As a result, your parent may want you to procrastinate, slow down in making a decision, not rush into something and manage your time in a better way. Time appears to be a major issue for parents and teenagers because they each have a schedule of activities and demands for the day.

No might mean there are too many things at one time

"No, you can't go to the party because you won't be back from church in time to go."

"No, you can't go to the play because you will be tired from the field day."

"No, you can't join the cheerleading squad because you will miss swim practice."

"No, don't join the chess club because it meets the same night as the golf club."

"No, it's impossible to go on the senior trip because you have to work and go to baseball practice."

No might mean you will be short on time

"No, if you watch television too late you won't have time to finish your homework."

"No, if you wait until Sunday night to start your project you won't be able to buy the supplies."

"No, if your group doesn't get together today, they won't have time to prepare the presentation."

"No, don't put off making your study guide or there won't be time to study for the test."

"No, you can't write the term paper on Sunday night or you won't have time to type the paper."

☙

No might mean something has already been scheduled

"No, you can't miss class because a test is scheduled for that day."

"No, you can't skip work to go to a party."

"No, you can't go to Mike's party because you already accepted an invitation to Ron's party."

"No, you can't take both classes because you won't have time to get across campus to the next class."

No, you aren't allowed to leave campus during the scheduled school day or you will be late for class when you return to campus."

No might mean there is a need to procrastinate

"No, don't pay the deposit until you are sure the housing is available."

"No, don't buy that computer; wait until you look at several different styles before you purchase it."

"No, don't sign up for summer school until you check the camp schedule."

"No, don't commit to the club officer board until you find out the demands and responsibilities of the board."

"No, don't sign up to organize a big event all by yourself, as you need helpers to complete such a big task."

No might mean you are making the decision too quickly

"No, don't go on a high risk climbing trip, think about the dangers of the trip."

"No, you can't go backpacking without your supplies or you could get stranded in the mountains."

"No, you can't go out in the heat without a water bottle as the water supply is limited in the work area."

"No, you can't go on a date with a person who is five years older than you, you are too young."

"No, you can't invite an extra friend on the trip because the seating is limited and the van only holds six people."

☙

No might mean there is a need to manage your time in a better way

"No, you can't go to a friend's house since you didn't unpack your suitcase from the last trip."

"No, you can't go to the party since you didn't clean your bedroom."

"No, you can't cook a big breakfast as you only have a few minutes to catch the bus."

"No, you can't wait to start a major project and expect to finish in a few hours."

"No, you can't go to the meeting on Wednesday night or you won't have time to study for the exam."

No might mean everything is a little too rushed

"No, don't walk so quickly as the sidewalk is covered with ice."

"No, don't rush into high risk sports without the proper training."

"No, don't go to the movie by yourself, wait for your friends."

"No, don't get on that go-cart, because Jake's uncle is still working on it and the brakes might not work."

"No, don't go so quickly in the school parking lot or you might get hit by a car."

No might mean you just need to wait

"No, you can't leave for the game until your Dad gets home."

"No, you aren't allowed to go in the stadium until the gates open."

"No, you can't leave without her, you have to wait until she buys her ticket and catches up with you."

"No, you can't go to the park until the class ends."

"No, you can't leave practice; you have to wait until the coach excuses you."

₈₀

No might mean there is bad timing in your request

"No, you can't go to the party until the house is cleaned."

"No, your father is sick and needs supervision, so you can't leave the house until he improves and he feels better."

"No, you can't go to the club because you need to babysit your sister."

"No, you can't play golf as it is raining and there could be a rain storm."

"No, you can't swim at night as there is no lifeguard on duty."

☙

No might mean not now, but at a later time

"No, you are not offered a scholarship at this time, but additional scholarships will be offered in the spring."

"No, you were not selected to the school leadership board, but additional board positions may be available in late May."

"No, you were not chosen for the basketball team, but you will be considered as an alternate for the team roster."

"No, you were not selected as a student in the Bio Med high school program, but you will be placed on a wait-list for future openings."

"No, you were not recognized for this year's award program, but your application will be considered in next year's competition."

CHAPTER THREE

No could mean there are complications

No could mean there are complications with your requests. Parents often say 'no' if they think the request is not a good fit, a bad idea, a no-win situation, an embarrassing situation or an unwise decision. They are often trying to warn you if you need to stop what you are doing or if there could be complications or road blocks ahead of you. Sometimes parents, teachers and adults are saying 'no' to check if you are delaying a task or putting off an important assignment. There are complications and very complicated situations in life and sometimes parents are just saying 'no' a conclusion cannot be reached.

No might mean it sounds like a bad idea

"No, you can't go, her car doesn't run well enough to take a long trip."

"No, the trip is too dangerous to take as there are snow storms on the interstate."

"No, you are not going to Hollywood alone, since you don't know anyone and don't have a place to stay."

"No, you can't go to New York, that is an expensive trip and you hardly have any money to pay for your expenses."

"No, the party is a bad idea right now because we have no money for food or drinks."

☙

No might mean you should just stop what you are doing

"No, don't go any further with the request because it is impossible to work out the extensive details."

"No, stop this behavior, it's hurting your friends and yourself."

"No, the plan for the party is ending right now as there are too many issues to address."

"No, the guest list is too big for a party in this small house so the party is cancelled."

"No, you cannot join the club because you are in too many clubs."

ಐ

No might mean it's a no-win situation

"No, there is no way to make up twenty missing assignments in one class period, it's just too late to play catch up."

"No, you can't run in a track meet with a broken leg."

"No, you should not run in a marathon when you haven't had the proper training and conditioning."

"No, you won't win if you sing in the contest with a hoarse voice."

"No, you can't perform the dance routine with a fever because you might faint."

☙

No might mean there could be a road block ahead of you

"No, you can't apply to the program until you take the prerequisites for the course."

"No, this application is sloppy and you won't be invited for an interview if they can't read the application."

"No, if you don't take the placement tests, you can't enroll in the program."

"No, don't enroll in the course, because you can't take courses in two schools at the same time."

"No, don't send in a poorly written essay or you won't be accepted into that college."

ಣ

No might mean there could be complications

"No, you can't talk on the phone for hours, it's distracting to your studies."

"No, you can't go out on Friday because you will be too tired for the track meet on Saturday morning."

"No, if you drive alone with your permit you could get a ticket and have higher insurance."

"No, don't wear that dress, it is too little and could tear easily."

"No, don't throw your trash out of the window or you could get a ticket for littering."

No might mean you are trying to cause delays

"No, stop putting off your research paper, you need to get started writing it."

"No, turn off the television and start making your study guide for the test."

"No, you can't go out tonight because you have to study for an exam in the morning."

"No, you are not ready to start the project because you haven't bought your supplies for the project."

"No, you can't turn that in, you need to organize the notebook before the notebook check tomorrow."

ଔ

No might mean that a conclusion has not been reached

"No, you didn't get picked in the first round of applicants, but there will be a second round of selections next week."

"No, the scholarships have been awarded this year, but sometimes additional funding comes open and we can offer more scholarships."

"No, your grades are not high enough for an academic scholarship, but we have other types of scholarships you may apply for this year."

"No, the state swim team has already been picked, but you can go as an alternate."

"No, you did not make the state gymnastics team, but you can compete in the individual events."

☙

No might mean a warning to prevent an embarrassing situation

"No, you can't dye your hair green, since it is not a natural color."

"No, you can't wear high heels on the mountain hiking trip or you will get blisters and have to take the shoes off your feet."

"No, you can't wear blue jeans and a flannel shirt to a formal occasion."

"No, don't text during the awards ceremony so you can focus on the speaker."

"No, you can't turn your phone on during class time."

No might mean it's an unwise decision

"No, you can't drop the course or you will lack credits for graduation."

"No, you will lose financial aid if you drop below twelve credits."

"No, you can't quit basketball or you will lose your chance at a sport's scholarship."

"No, you can't drive with friends in the car or you might jeopardize your driver's license."

"No, you can' drive the car without insurance because you could have a wreck and that would be a big expense."

ଔ

No might mean it is not a good fit

"No, the travel plans won't work because there will be no time to get to the performance."

"No, if you go to the movie, you can't get to the skating rink before it closes."

"No, don't take the bus or you will miss the flight."

"No, don't stay up late or you will miss your ride early in the morning."

"No, don't move tonight or you will be late for work in the morning."

ଚଓ

CHAPTER FOUR
No could mean it's not really appropriate

No could mean that what you are requesting is not really appropriate. Parents and adults may be helping you to understand that certain behaviors are not appropriate or acceptable and that it is not appropriate to proceed with the request. They may be helping you to understand that stress will be too high or a load will be too heavy. Sometimes there is not enough lapse time between two activities to complete them both. Parents and teachers may be giving you a warning that you are too challenging to other people, speaking out of turn or lying to cover up the truth. On the other hand, parents could be warning you someone else could be trying to take advantage of you.

No might mean it's not appropriate to proceed at this time

"No, you can't stay after school because there is a flash flood warning and the weather report indicates it's a dangerous situation."

"No, the end times of the classes overlap, so you can't enroll in the Spanish class."

"No, you can't try out for cheerleading because you are having knee surgery."

"No, you can't sign up for the driving test because you are not old enough."

"No, you can't go to the state camp as the car is broken down."

No might mean that someone could take advantage of you

"No, you are not allowed to give the study guide to Dana because you won't have anything to study for the test."

"No, you can't loan money to John, he has no way to pay you back."

"No, you can't give your backpack to Jane as you will have nothing to use to carry your school books."

"No, you can't loan Jennifer the prom dress or you will have nothing to wear to the dance."

"No, if you pay for all his gas you will have no money for food."

No might mean you are challenging other people

"No, you can't call your teacher a name or you will be suspended from school."

"No, you cannot tell the coach he is wrong or you won't get any playing time."

"No, you can't bad mouth your team mates or you could be kicked off of the team."

"No, you can't criticize the teacher because you don't like the way he dresses or it could cost your grade."

"No, you can't say ugly things to your instructor, because you need a scholarship recommendation."

ೞ

No might mean that you are lying to cover up the truth

"No, you can't be in two places at one time- either you are at tutoring or the movies."

"No, you aren't studying for the test if you are at baseball practice."

"No, you were not at Mary's house because I called and no one was at home."

"No, you did not attend class today, because your teacher called me."

"No, you did not go to basketball practice on Monday because your coach told me that you missed practice."

No might mean you are trying to speak out of turn

"No, you cannot make a complaint for everyone, you can only make an individual complaint."

"No, stop complaining, you need to write a letter expressing your unique concerns with the class."

"No, you can't tell her what to do- it's her own personal decision."

"No, you can't speak for the whole class; you should only express your personal concerns."

"No, you can't make a complaint when you haven't fully researched all of the issues and know the views of the group."

ଓ

No might mean the load is too heavy

"No, don't take both classes or you will never have free time."

"No, don't take two English classes or there will be too much strain on your eyes from reading a large amount of information."

"No, those two history classes will be too difficult to take in the Spring."

"No, you can't be in four clubs and on the swim team or you will be stressed out."

"No, the part time job is not a good idea or your grades will suffer this semester.

> **No might mean there is not a time lapse between events**

"No, you can't leave the swim meet after regionals because the state meet starts immediately after the regional events."

"No, you can't leave early because the awards ceremony will follow the pageant finals."

"No, you can't skip rehearsal because it is the night before the talent show."

"No, you can't miss football practice because it is right before the homecoming game."

"No, you can't forget to take your clothes as you need to change before the awards reception."

☙

No might mean the stress will be too high

"No, don't over commit to more than one club or the demands will be too great."

"No, don't try out for dance team as you haven't developed the skills to compete at that elite level."

"No, don't tell friends you will win because the competition is very tough."

"No, don't go to the try-outs until you warm up for the competition."

"No, don't take such a heavy load of classes because your grades could suffer."

ೞ

No might mean it is not appropriate

"No, you can't wear shorts to the graduation because it is a formal event."

"No, you can't go without a shirt to a wedding, it's a formal occasion."

"No, you shouldn't take five cookies off of the plate, it is better to take one or two cookies until the others are served."

"No, you shouldn't stuff your mouth with food or you might spit up food at the table."

"No, you can't talk on the phone in church as it interrupts the service."

No might mean your behavior is unacceptable

"No, you cannot hit people when you are upset or angry."

"No, you cannot force others to wait on you, when you are watching television."

"No, you cannot make strong demands that are self centered and uncaring."

"No, you can't leave dirty dishes on the table, each person has to help with clean up."

"No, your trash must be picked up as littering in the park is unacceptable."

ଛ

CHAPTER FIVE
No could mean there are safety issues

No could mean there are safety issues your parents and teachers want you to consider. Sometimes parents and adults want to say "no" to give a safety caution, to give you a warning or to protect you from harm. Basically, parents are concerned with the motives of others. They want you to be aware of the threat of danger and helping you to avoid future danger. Teachers and parents want you to think about the potential cost of the risks and be aware when the risks are high or circumstances are risky.

No might mean the risks are not worth the cost

"No, don't take football or you might get an injury that would ruin your future track career."

"No, don't take all hard courses or you might ruin your GPA."

"No, if you don't participate in the state track meet you could limit your chances of getting the scholarship."

"No, don't goof off on your classes or you will forfeit the scholarship."

"No, don't avoid the deadlines or your application will be late for acceptance into college."

No might mean there is a potential risk

"No, you can't wear a pointed gage ear ring on a roller coaster ride or you might tear your ear."

"No, you shouldn't pierce your tongue as it might chip the enamel off of the back of your teeth."

"No, you can't walk home alone because it is an unsafe situation."

"No, you can't leave a wound unprotected as you could get an infection if you don't clean the cut."

"No, you can't go by yourself in the mall; it is unsafe to stray away from the group of kids."

No might mean the circumstances are risky

"No, you are not allowed to ride the horse because you are recovering from surgery."

"No, the odds are not in your favor of passing if you take the more difficult class first."

"No, you can't take the intermediate class because you could get hurt; go back to the beginner class."

"No, I can't allow you to take the car since I don't have insurance on it."

"No, you can't take the advanced ski slope until you check out the beginner slopes."

☙

No might mean to be cautious of some people's motives

"No, you can't go inside that building, it is very unsafe to go with people you don't know well."

"No, don't accept a ride from someone you don't know."

"No, you are not allowed to go with a group of kids that are not from your school."

"No, you can't go with her since I have not met her family or parents."

"No, you can't go because you have not told me what your plans are for tonight."

No might mean there could be future damage

"No, don't listen to loud music or you could damage your ear drum."

"No, don't have sex with your boyfriend as you could regret it later."

"No, don't break your commitment to the club as you might want to run for club officer at a later time."

"No, don't leave the picnic until you help clean up and do your part as it makes you look irresponsible to leave without helping."

"No, don't quit your job, you need to work longer to gain some more job experience."

ଞ

No might mean there is a safety caution

"No, stop playing on the tree or you might fall hard to the ground."

"No, stop playing ball in the street or you could get hit by a car."

"No, you shouldn't speed in a school zone as there are many children around and some child could get hit by the car."

"No, you can't go barefoot on the hiking trail or you might cut your foot."

"No, stop stuffing or you could choke if you put too much food in your mouth."

No might mean the risks are too high

"No, skateboarding fast, because a sprain or break could be very serious and could cause you to have a lifelong injury."

"No, you can't compete in gymnastics until you take the beginning skills course."

"No, you can't go to the next level until you take the safety exam."

"No, you can't break dance on a hard tile floor because you could get hurt."

"No, you can't ride the motorcycle or the go-cart until your leg fully heals."

No might mean that you are being protected from harm

"No, you can't get into a car with a guy you don't know."

"No, that girl wants you to loan her money that you will never see again."

"No, you can't go to an unsupervised birthday party with no adults around the house."

"No, you are not allowed to stay late after high school to talk with friends when there are no clubs or tutoring."

"No, you can't invite a girl over to watch a movie when your parents are at work."

No might mean there is a threat of danger

"No, you can't go sell candy door to door by yourself or you could get kidnapped."

"No, you aren't allowed to ride the motorcycle without a helmet or you could get a head injury."

"No, you can't go to the movie without taking your cell phone or you won't have a way to call for pick up after the late show."

"No, you can't get on the skateboard ramp without wrist and knee pads or you will sprain or break something."

"No, you can't go hiking if you don't take a water bottle with you."

☙

No might mean you could put yourself in a dangerous situation

"No, don't stay in the dorm room alone, you need to stay with your room-mate for safety."

"No, going up Elm Street could put you in danger as there are roadblocks down to one lane."

"No, the weather report is not good for driving to the beach."

"No, don't drive, the streets are flooded so just stay at your aunt's house."

"No, don't stay late at school because there is not a security guard on duty."

ଔ

No might mean there is a warning

"No, don't go swimming; the temperature is too cold to swim in the morning."

"No, don't take the interstate because there was a pile-up thirty minutes ago and the traffic is stalled."

"No, don't take the job working outside, because the temperatures are in the 100's this week."

"No, that school is too far away from the airport for you to make your flight."

"No, don't go on the road trip up in the mountains where the roads are curvy and narrow."

☙

CHAPTER SIX
No could mean the request is not a good resource

No could mean it is not a good resource for you. Parents want you to think about your resources by considering if items are economical for you, if purchases are out of your budget or are high dollar items. Parents and teachers want you to consider how to be resourceful by checking out your options as you give more consideration to your request and choices. They don't want you to limit your potential, but understand that some tasks are complicated and you may not always be making the best decision.

No might mean it is not economical at this time

"No, you can't have the money for the yearbook until I get paid again."

"No, you won't be able to get the car until you save for the down payment."

"No, you can't go to the movies until you clean your room and earn an allowance."

"No, I can't pay for the trip, but you can babysit and work part time to earn the money for the travel expenses."

"No, you can't buy the class ring until you save the money you earn from the job."

No might mean it is a bad budget item

"No, you can't get a new phone every time there is an upgrade as the price is too high."

"No, you can't buy a new computer because your old computer works fine."

"No, you can't buy a $1000.00 prom dress; the family budget won't allow it."

"No, you can't afford a high dollar car when you have very little money."

"No, you shouldn't buy that expensive purse since you are also trying to save for the senior trip."

No might mean you need to be a better consumer

"No, you can't buy new jeans every week of the school year; you can wear them for longer periods of time."

"No, you can't have a new dress for every dance; the dress can be worn more than once."

"No, you can't spend every dime you earn; you need to open a savings account."

"No, you can't buy the skateboard; you need to save the money for the car."

"No, you can't afford to pay separately for the tickets when it is cheaper to buy a combo package."

ଞ

No might mean you aren't making the best decision

"No, you can't drop out of school, because you don't have a better road to take right now."

"No, you can't fail the class or it will delay your graduation from high school."

"No, you aren't allowed to participate in high risk sports before you go to training camp."

"No, you can't get in trouble or you could get arrested before the team selections are made."

"No, you can't drive your friends to the dance because you could get a ticket and lose your driving permit."

☏

No might mean some tasks are very complicated

"No, you can't text your friends when you need to sew the project."

"No, you can't play around when it takes hours to study for the test."

"No, you aren't allowed to talk on the phone when you need to research your term paper."

"No, you can't slack off because a homecoming float takes a lot of workers."

"No, you can't leave early because you need to volunteer at the football concession stand."

No might mean you are not being resourceful

"No, don't throw away the scraps of material, we can use them more wisely as we make the quilt for the competition."

"No, don't toss the pop tops as the school is collecting them for a fund raiser."

"No, don't throw out the meat; we can use it for a casserole."

"No, don't pour out the broth; we can use it for the chicken soup."

"No, don't throw out the onion; we can use it when we make the salad."

‽

No might mean you are limiting your potential

"No, don't take the easy path, because the more difficult path has many rewards in the end."

"No, don't enroll in such an easy course, when your skill levels are higher."

"No, don't go the beginner route when you can clearly enter at the intermediate or advanced route."

"No, don't audition for the novice division when your skill level is in the gifted range."

"No, don't go to the beginning swim camp when your skills are at the elite level."

≈

No might mean there could be more consideration of the request

"No, you can't sign the contract since you haven't read the fine print."

"No, you can't get a car loan until you fill out the papers and they check your credit."

"No, you can't commit to both college scholarships, you need to check out the colleges and decide which one you like more."

"No, you aren't allowed to play on two high school teams at the same time; it is against the district regulations."

"No, you can't compete in two choral divisions or you will break competition rules."

☙

No might mean there is a need to check out more options

"No, don't sign up so quickly until you check out the other clubs."

"No, don't enroll in the class until you check out the entire list of classes."

"No, don't go volunteer so fast until you check out the details of the project."

"No, don't commit to one job until you go to both of the interviews to check out different part time jobs."

"No, you can't take a full time job while you are in school, you need to explore part-time jobs."

No might mean it is out of your budget

"No, those jeans are $200.00, find a cheaper pair."

"No, the movie popcorn is too much; you will have to share with your sister."

"No, you can't buy four clothing items, when you only have the money for two items."

"No, the shoes are too expensive and they look at little small so you will probably grow out of them too fast."

"No, you can't afford those tickets for the front row seats, the back rows are cheaper."

CHAPTER SEVEN
No could mean there is no clear direction

No could mean there is no clear direction in life. Parents and teachers are trying to help you realize there are guidelines to follow and when there are limitations and boundaries in life. They want to help you when you are unclear about your plans, when you are in unknown territory and when you need to take small steps in life. Overall, they want to help you take responsibility for your actions, to help you look at your choices, to get your priorities in order and to look at issues that could impact future events for you.

No might mean the other person is unclear about your plans

"No, you can't go if your friend doesn't ask her parents to drive you all."

"No, you are not going to a party without a formal invitation."

"No, you can't go to the play with friends because you don't know what time it begins or ends."

"No, you are not going up to the lakes and a cabin without providing the address from his parents."

"No, you can't go to the dance without giving me the name and phone number of your date."

No might mean there is unknown territory ahead of you

"No, don't go on this trip because you have not estimated the mileage or mapped out the directions."

"No, you can't move into the apartment because you have not checked out the neighborhood."

"No, don't get the car because you don't have money for the future car payments and the insurance."

"No, you can't move in with those room-mates because you don't know them well enough."

"No, you can't move to Los Angeles without a job or money."

No might mean that you need to look at other choices

"No, don't make a quick decision, look at all your options."

"No, don't commit so soon since other teams are trying to recruit you."

"No, don't sign the scholarship acceptance letter until you have checked out several colleges and programs."

"No, don't make a big decision until you discuss it with your counselor."

"No, don't tell the recruiter 'yes' until you talk it over with your family."

No might mean you need to get your priorities in order

"No, don't pack your suitcase until you read the camp supply list and organize the needed supplies for the trip."

"No, don't buy school supplies until you get the class syllabus."

"No, you can't jump into the advanced typing class until you take the basic typing class."

"No, the computer program won't work until you have installed the updates."

"No, you can't write a term paper until you have read the research on the topic."

☙

No might mean it will impact a future event

"No, you can't go to the Bible study because it gets out too late and you have a Spanish test early in the morning."

"No, you can't commit to late night activities because you have an early schedule every morning."

"No, if you don't go to the early morning workout you won't be ready for the track meet."

"No, you can't miss school or the truant officer will come out and investigate."

"No, you can't skip the course review or it will impact your test score on the exam."

No might mean there are guidelines to follow

"No, you can't drive the car until you pass the driving test."

"No, you can't go on the hiking tour until you wear long pants, a jacket and closed toed shoes."

"No, your signature is not acceptable unless you use a black or blue pen."

"No, you were not accepted in medical camp because your application was received after the deadline date."

"No, you forgot to sign the contract so it will be invalid."

No might mean there are some boundaries

"No, you can't walk all over the airport, stay at the gate or assigned area."

"No, you can't scuba dive in the water without the proper skill training and scuba certifications."

"No, you can't go down West Street unless you walk with a buddy because safety is a big issues in that area."

"No, it was not a good ball as the serve was over the line."

"No, you are in the wrong area as the sign states "no trespassing."

No might mean there are some limitations

"No, you can't be in the ballet dance group because you rehearsed with the tap dancers."

"No, you can't be the goalie in the soccer game, because you missed practice."

"No, you are not eligible to apply because your test scores were too low."

"No, we only take the first 100 applications, so you will need to reapply in the spring."

"No, you can't buy it because there is a cut off and a financial limit to how much you can spend on the credit card."

No might mean you need to take small steps

"No, don't skip the basic course or you could have difficulty as the courses get harder."

"No, don't jump to the advanced team since you lack the technique to compete at the level."

"No, don't hop around to different courses when you need to complete the graduation requirements first."

"No, don't pass up the opportunity to take the course since you can't advance in the program without the first foundation course."

"No, don't jump from team to team when you need to show the coach you are a committed player."

ଔ

No might mean it is time for you to take responsibility for your actions

"No, you can't go to soccer because you misplaced your soccer gear."

"No, you aren't allowed to invite friends over until you put away your clothes and clean up your room."

"No, you are not prepared to leave for camp because you forgot to do the laundry."

"No, you cannot get in the house unless you put the key in your backpack."

"No, you can't go to the mall if you don't take money to pay for your own lunch and expenses."

CHAPTER EIGHT
No could mean more reflection is needed

No could mean that more reflection is needed on your request. Parents sometimes want you to just give a second thought and reflect on an event. This might involve slowing down and thinking about your plans, rethinking a position or thinking before you act on something. No might mean that you need to be corrected on some facts or there is a tangle in your plans. Sometimes parents and teachers are letting you see that reflection is needed because you need to change a path or the steps are too big.

No might mean to give something a second thought

"No, you can't have a tattoo, it is long lasting, so think about your decision and the change in your skin."

"No, you can't lay in the sun for hours, think about how it could damage your skin."

"No, you can't go, it is risky to ride with someone who just got their license."

"No, you are not allowed to attend the concert because you don't meet the age requirement."

"No, you cannot go to a party where alcohol is served, since it is illegal to drink when you are underage."

☙

No might mean there is a need to reflect on something

"No, don't hit your sister, how do you feel if someone hits you?"

"No, don't shoot the rubber band in his face, you could cause permanent blindness in his eye."

"No, you can't go with that group of friends as I sense there might be trouble."

"No, you can't go out with Pat, I don't have a good feeling about this."

"No, you can't ride with a group of kids in that small car-it is over the limit and is unsafe."

> **No might mean you need to think before you act on a situation**

"No, think about the consequences of dating two guys at the same time."

"No, if you join the French club you will have a conflict with math tutoring."

"No, if you make a down payment on the car you will not have enough for the course registration."

"No, don't spend the money at the mall because you need it for the senior trip."

"No, don't add the class or your course load will be too heavy."

ഔ

No might mean you need to be correct on the facts

"No, you can't be admitted to the program until you read the catalog and complete the application process."

"No, you're mistaken in thinking that you can skip steps in the registration process."

"No, recruitment doesn't happen that fast, the recruitment procedures are strict and it is a long process."

"No, the scholarship is not without stipulations, you must keep your grade point average up to maintain the scholarship."

"No, the students at the private high school do not wear uniforms, but there is a specific dress code."

No might mean there is a need to rethink a position

"No, don't take the North road as there is a lot of construction in that part of town."

"No, don't go out for soccer and football, if you try out for two sports it could be taxing on your body."

"No, don't lift that heavy box-get a dolly or you could injure your back."

"No, slow down and think about those risky moves in cheerleading or you might get hurt."

"No, you can't write that in your report or it might be misinterpreted."

No might mean there is a tangle in the plans

"No, you can't pick up Kathy and Dana at the same time-they live across town from each other."

"No, you can't drive to the game first because it is too far away from the school."

"No, you can't make the doctor's appointment the same time as the dress rehearsal-it won't work out."

"No, you can't participate in the recital and the science fair because they are in the same night."

"No, you can't eat a hamburger because you are allergic to beef."

ଔ

No might mean it's time to change your path

"No, the baseball team might not be a good choice since you have trouble running and putting support on your right foot."

"No, you don't have to study in the medical program if your heart is not in it."

"No, you don't have to take the technical route as you could choose the artistic coursework."

"No, you don't have to study dance if your dream is to be a singer."

"No, you don't have to be so specific about picking your major as there are many different careers in one field."

☙

No might mean that it is not a good solution

"No, you can't take the late bus or you will miss dance practice."

"No, you can't walk to Jill's house because there are barriers and you would have to cross a dangerous intersection."

"No, you can't wait at the bus stop by yourself-it is just too dangerous."

"No, you can't ride the motorcycle in heavy traffic or you could be in a bad accident."

"No, you can't lift that heavy weight set or you could hurt your back."

No might mean the steps are too big

"No, you can't jump to the advanced course until you take the introduction course."

"No, you won't be able to take the driving test until you study the driving manual and get your permit."

"No, you can't take the exam until you take the review course."

"No, you won't make the high school team until you get experience on the middle school team."

"No, you can't jump from a beginner into the elite swim team without attending the summer advanced swim session."

☙

No might mean to slow down and think about future plans

"No, you don't have the money to rent the apartment, so stay at home until you save the money."

"No, you can't buy the car till you save the money for the down payment and car title."

"No, you can't apply to that college until you take your exams."

"No, you can't apply to the program until you mail in the official transcripts."

"No, the deadline is closed for this year, but you can apply for next year."

CHAPTER NINE
No could mean learning new lessons

No could mean that you're just learning new lessons. This is often based on your parent's experiences and they really want to help you learn new lessons. Parents and adults may simply be saying 'no' because something is not good for you, you lack the skills for something or you are just learning a lesson for yourself. The parents want to help you avoid missing a deadline or an opportunity when you don't speak up for yourself. These adults want to help you distinguish if there is a better solution or if a better opportunity awaits you. Parents may also say 'no' because they are proud of you and accept you as a person.

No might mean you missed a deadline

"No, you were not accepted into the magnet school because your application was one hour late."

"No, you cannot attend camp because the deadline to apply has passed."

"No, you cannot apply for the internship because the deadline was last week."

"No, you cannot be accepted into the summer program because the deadline has passed and will not open until next year."

"No, you will not be allowed to participate in graduation because the course was completed too late."

No might mean you are not speaking up for yourself

"No, I will not email your teacher, she wants you to go talk to her about the grade."

"No, I will not call his mother- you two need to work this out between yourselves."

"No, I won't tell her, you need to tell her that she can't borrow the money."

"No, you can't go to the party because you didn't ask for the details of the party."

"No, you are not allowed to take the course because you did not get permission from your instructor to take it."

No might mean a better opportunity awaits you

"No, you didn't make the football team, but the coach of the track team wants to talk with you."

"No, you didn't get the scholarship to the private school, but the advanced technology school wants to recruit you."

"No, you weren't picked from the cheerleader try-outs, but your talent agent wants you to audition for a commercial."

"No, you didn't make the state play offs, but there is still a chance you could be picked as a wild card entry."

"No, you weren't picked for state choir, but you were selected as an alternate in the district choir."

No might mean you need to do what is good for you

"No, you can't skip swimming lessons because you need to condition your body to get ready for the meet."

"No, you can't stop your daily routine because you need the exercise."

"No, you can't skip meals or your energy level will go down."

"No, you can't lay in bed all day or you will gain weight."

"No, you can't be mean and hurt others, you need to apologize and make things right so you both feel good."

☙❧

No might mean that your parents are proud of you

"No, you didn't have the winning score, but you gave it your best try."

"No, you didn't win the game, but you made the last two field goals showing a great effort."

"No, you can't always make the team, but you showed good sportsmanship."

"No, you didn't win the tennis match, but I liked the way you shook her hand to congratulate her."

"No, you weren't the best performer, but you gave a strong performance and people noticed your talent."

No might mean that your parents accept you

"No, you didn't win the prize, but you were one of the most talented performers."

"No, you didn't sell the most brownies at the bake sale, but I like the way you organized the booth."

"No, you didn't get the scholarship at your favorite college, but I am sure another college will offer you a scholarship."

"No, you won't play football in college because of the injury, but we know another career path will open up for you."

"No, you don't have the Math skills to get in the program, but we will help you find another program that fits you better."

No might mean there is a need for a different solution

"No don't go to the movies, because you need to be at play rehearsal around seven o'clock."

"No, don't invite two friends since there is only room in the car for one more person."

"No, you can't invite everyone to the party because we are limited to ten movie tickets."

"No, the basketball camp is too expensive, but you can go to a similar camp with a lower registration fee."

"No, you can't go to both camps because you would be exhausted and tired, but you can pick the one camp you would most prefer to attend."

☙

No might mean you lack the skills in an area

"No, you did not pass the exam criteria of typing 25 words per minute as a minimum of 50 words per minute is required for the job."

"No, you did not get the part in the play, you must have completed the advanced dance performance class."

"No, we were unable to consider you for the teen editor position because you lack school newspaper experience."

"No, you were not considered for the part-time job because you lack fast food experience."

"No, you were not selected for the honors class, because your grades were not high enough in the regular program of study."

No might mean there was never any real opportunity

"No, you were not selected for the teen leadership position as the position has been closed due to lack of funds."

"No, further review of your scholarship application has been suspended due to the fact the department is closing."

"No, you were not picked for the league as we have terminated spring training."

"No, your drawing was not selected as the illustration company is closing next spring."

"No, your team application was not considered because the program was discontinued and combined with a new program."

ଔ

No might mean learning a new lesson

"No, you did not make an A, because you did not complete the extra credit assignments."

"No, you did not pass the class because you failed to dress up in sports attire for daily practice."

"No, you lost the part in the play since you did not attend rehearsals."

"No, you can't keep the car because you did not make the car payments."

"No, you can't keep the appointment as you were an hour late and your appointment has been cancelled."

ଔ

RECOMMENDED READING FOR TEENAGERS

Carlson, R. (2000). *Don't sweat the small stuff for teens: simple ways to keep cool in stressful times.* New York: Hyperion.

Covey, S. (1998). *The 7 habits of highly effective teens.* New York: Touchstone.

Graham, S. (2000). *Teens can make it happen.* New York: Touchstone.

Shipp, Josh (2010). *The teen's guide to world domination: Advice on life, liberty and pursuit of awesomeness.* New York: St. Martin's Griffin.

McGraw, J. (2000). *Life strategies for teens.* New York: Touchstone.

INDEX

A
Actions, 77
Adjustments, 6
Advantage, 36
Appropriate, 34-35, 43

B
Bad habits, 5
Bad idea, 24
Behavior, 44
Boundaries, 75
Budget, 59, 67

C
Calm down, 3
Caution, 51
Change, 1, 85
Challenges, 10
Challenging, 37
Choices, 71
Complicated, 62
Complications, 23, 28, 37
Conclusion, 30
Confusion, 9
Consumer, 60

D
Danger, 54
Damage, 50
Deadline, 91
Decision, 17, 32, 61
ys, 29
, 9
, 68

E
Economical, 58
Embarrassing situation, 31

F
Facts, 83
Fit, 33
Future event, 73

G
Good, 94
Guidelines, 74

H
Habits, 5
Heavy load, 40

I
Idea, 24
Independence, 7
Inflexible, 4

L
Lapse, 41
Lesson, 100
Lessons, 90
Limitations, 76
Load, 40
Lying, 38

M
Motives, 49

N
No-Win Situation, 26

O
Opportunity, 93, 99
Options, 2, 66

P
Parents, 95-96, 102

Path, 86
Plans, 10, 69, 85, 89
Potential, 64
Priorities, 72
Procrastinate, 16
Protect, 53
Proud, 95
Q
Quickly, 17
R
Reflect, 81
Reflection, 79
Relationship, 8
Relax, 3
Resource, 57
Resourceful, 63
Responsibility, 78
Request, 11, 65
Rethink, 84
Risk, 47
Risks, 46, 52
Risky, 48
Roadblock, 27
Rushed, 19
S
Safety, 45, 51
Scheduled, 15
Situation, 26, 82
Skills, 98
Slowdown, 8
Solution, 87, 97
Small steps, 77
Speak out of turn, 39

Speaking up, 92
Steps, 87
Stop, 25
Stress, 42
T
Tangle, 85
Think, 81
Thought, 79
Threat, 54
Time, 13-14, 18, 22, 41, 57
Timing 12, 21
Truth, 38
U
Unacceptable, 44
Unclear, 68
Unhealthy, 11
Unknown territory, 69
Unwise decision, 32
W
Wait, 20
Warning, 31, 56

ABOUT THE AUTHOR

Susan Louise Peterson has devoted most of her career to working with students as a school psychologist, writer and public school educator. She has seen students struggle with emotional and behavioral concerns when not understanding why their teachers and parents are responding to their requests and demands in a negative way with the word 'no.'

Susan is the author of books like, *Why Children Make Up Stories: A Practical Guide to Help Adults Recognize the Underlying Reasons Children Make-Up Stories* (International Scholars Publications) and *Is My Child Autistic or Delayed?* (Vilnius Press) as well as other books in the areas of education and research. Susan has lived in Las Vegas, NV for more than 20 years. She spends her free time with her husband and twin daughters who often hear the word 'no' in response to their requests.

uct-compliance